I BELONG
TO
NOWHERE

POEMS OF HOPE
AND RESISTANCE

TRANSLATED BY

I BELONG TO NOWHERE

POEMS OF HOPE AND RESISTANCE

KALYANI THAKUR CHARAL

SIPRA MUKHERJEE
MRINMOY PRAMANICK

TILTED AXIS PRESS

CONTENTS

From *The Girl Who Tracks the Dark /*
Je Meye Andhar Gone

From *Chandalini's Poetry /*
Chandalinir Kabita

From *Every Night Knows /*
Protiti Ratri Jane

Kalyani likes calling a spade a spade. So when she found
people treating her with condescension disguised as civil-
ity, and all because she belonged to a lowered caste group,
she decided to speak their unspoken discrimination into
her name. She is from the Dalit community that used to be
called Chandals, a name that the community had rejected
through the 1911 Census when they decided to name
themselves Namasudras. Caste discrimination itself has been
forbidden by the Constitution that independent India gave
itself in 1950. But there were many who remained hung
up on the past and could not wrap their heads around the
idea of equality enshrined in this Constitution. For them,
the Namasudra was still the Chandal. In fact, even the word
'Chandal' could be too much to pronounce for those who
looked down upon Kalyani's community. For these people,
the word 'Chandal' would be distorted into 'Chadal', or
'Charal'. So Kalyani added it to her name. If that was the
first thing people thought of when they met her, but could
not speak it, she would speak it for them. She introduces
herself therefore as Kalyani Thakur Charal.

Literacy and education were hard-won achievements for
Kalyani. Born to a family that was closely connected with

the Matua religious movement, she imbibed the doctrines of this sect that had demanded human dignity and respect and resisted Brahminical hierarchy since the late nineteenth century. Her father was a feminist who worked first in the jute trade, then in the rice trade, and also as a security guard at night as he tried to give his children the best education. Her mother Renuka was a quietly determined woman with an irrepressible thirst for education. She took care of the home, tended the farming land they had and stayed up into the night parboiling the paddy grains. Sometimes she sent Kalyani off with a basket full of vegetables and fruits from their patch of land. Kalyani would carry the basket to the railway station not far from their house and sell them. She remembers the women of the locality sitting around her mother with their kantha stitchings in the afternoons, after the day's cooking was done. Renuka would read out from the Matua books they had at home. These were the only books they had at home.

Kalyani moved to the city of Calcutta, now Kolkata, for her higher education. After her graduation, she worked for the Indian Railways for 27 years, learning to negotiate the viciousness and cruelty that humans so casually heap on one another. Her autobiography Ami Keno Charal Likhi (Why I Write Charal) which won the Sparrow Literary Award in 2017, was born out of her experiences of these years in the city. Having fought her way out of the margins and into the mainstream, Kalyani was here frequently perceived as 'different'.

Among the many books she has written and the journals she edits, is one slim volume of a journal that Kalyani publishes regularly. This is a journal called Neer (also transliterated as 'Needh', meaning 'nest' or 'home'). Though a writer-activist against discrimination faced by her Dalit caste community, this journal brings within its covers writings by many Adivasi writers too, the indigenous people of the Indian subcontinent. This journal is an interesting project of hers which began as a wall magazine when she came to stay in the city at a hostel for working women. Over time, it has metamorphosed into a full grown journal through which Kalyani tries to re-collect the communities' folklores or arts or highlight issues such as the refugee situation, women in the city or water crisis. She is also closely connected with the Dalit publishing house, Chaturtha Duniya (The Fourth World), set up by West Bengal's Dalits and housed in Stall 22 on Calcutta's College Street, a four-feet by-three-feet cupboard-stall which they open every Thursday evening after returning from work.

Kalyani stays and works in the city of Kolkata now, having created a home of her own there. She travels frequently to her hometown of Bagula in the Nadia district and has recently set up a library there, named after her mother who passed on at 45 years of age, the Renuka Thakur Dalit Granthagar.

AN ANGER ANCHORED IN CRITICAL REFLEXIVITY ANIMATES KALYANI THAKUR'S POEMS

Kaushal Panwar

My first encounter with Kalyani Thakur Charal Ji was in Nagpur, at the All India Dalit Women's Conference, which I had the privilege of inaugurating. In the evening, after the program, a group of us got together including professor Hemlata Mahishwar, Sanjiv Chandan, Kalyani Thakur and one more individual whose name I'm unable to recall now. We all travelled by car to the Mahatma Gandhi International Hindi University, Wardha, at the behest of the Student's Union there to address a conference on Savitribai Phule. It was in that conference that I heard Kalyani Thakur Ji speaking for the first time. In spite of the linguistic differences between us, the essence of her address infused with the ideas of Jotirao Phule and Babasaheb Ambedkar was both memorable and powerful. I recall she also recited a poem of hers in her formal address to the audience. Thereafter, the students posed several questions to the three of us on stage, which, I recall, made the conference proceedings intensely meaningful. Then they all requested for more poems to be recited. I distinctly remember the poems from Kalyani Ji's *Chandalinir Kabita* echoing in the air that evening. Prior to this, I had only encountered Kalyani Ji whilst reading her poetry and following her passionate activism towards humanist and feminist causes.

It is often said that literature is a mirror of the social world. However, in actuality, what that 'literature' reflects is a painfully partial reality; it excises the experiences of that part of India that lives with its voices, stories, memories and debilities silenced in dominant literary canons. In order that this 'hidden India' can truly be reflected in the mirror that is literature there emerged, from the mid 20th century, a distinctive stream of 'Dalit literature', which today is being read, researched and taught in every corner of India, and even around the world. For the sake of understanding, we can say Dalit literature originated in 1958 from the Dalit Panthers. That which the labels 'Untouchable', 'Harijan' and 'Atishudra' couldn't encompass – as identities imposed from above on India's 'lower castes' – was what the self-claimed identity Dalit Panther embodied and became. The Dalit Panthers worked extensively and astutely with Babasaheb Ambedkar's idea(l)s. During Ambedkar's time the foundational framework of Dalit literature was being prepared in Nagpur. It was there, around 1958, that a manifesto of Dalit literature was first written-up in the Marathi language. About two decades later it was in the same language (Marathi) that the All India Dalit Movement was established, which began galvanizing support for Dalits and even spread to neighbouring Gujarat. Around the same time, in the late 70s, the Dalit Sangharsh Samiti (DSS) came up in Karnataka and became a formidable collective of Dalit authors, poets, activists and storytellers. In this way, from the mid 20th century onwards, Dalit literature gradually began to be written in every corner of the country. Irrigated by the ideas of

Ambedkar and Phule it even spread eastwards to Bengal. Bengali Literature has always had its own particular characteristics, which makes it distinct from the other literatures of India. Yet, in its flourishing, this new literature elaborated and expanded on the Ambedkarite Dalit literature first written in Marathi. The historical, political and literary arc of Dalit literature in India is thus wide and varied and is ever expanding even today, bleeding into the bounds of 'Tribal/Indigenous literature', 'Subaltern literature' and establishing all-along a vital, humanistic readership, resonance and reach for itself.

When Dalit literature was in its formative years, it wasn't an uncommon (albeit Brahmanically casteist) assumption that this literature drawn from the experiences of the marginalized castes wouldn't last long and would soon fade away. Since it was not seen to be 'scientific' and 'rational', and was considered 'sans ideology', such stereotypes marred the existence and acceptance of Dalit literature in the so-called 'mainstream'. From today's vantage, however, Dalit literature has not only obliterated such Brahmanical assumptions but also forced a radical reckoning with their deeper social, cultural, political, psychological and existential underpinnings. The composite, cross-genre literary work happening under the rubric of Dalit literature today is not only self-reflexive (shedding critical light on the multi-layered experiences of India's Dalit communities themselves) but equally robust in its capacity to interrogate the myriad nuances of savarna society, including highlighting the possibilities of building solidarities between oppressed peoples across the world. As it rescripts Dalit identity by drawing attention to the complexities of caste(ism) – including what Ambedkar called caste's 'graded inequalities' – Dalit literature also radically (re)defines the ambit of humanistic socio-developmental agendas anew. In the initial years, the literature of the oppressed castes came from villages, then it rapidly started taking root in cities and urban areas. In the contemporary context women Dalit writers have come into the core of this multifarious, anti-caste literary production in significant ways. In this manner, Dalit literature is finding several new interlocutors and capaciously creating intersections with the peoples and principles of other social movements dealing with issues like anti-racism, anti capitalism, feminism, sexuality, trans-rights etc.

From the second decade of the 20th century, the term 'Dalit' – which literally means 'broken' and 'ground down' – came to be used not as a slur signifying oppression but as a symbol of radical hope and aspiration. As early as 1914, Hira Dom, who is credited with writing and publishing the first Dalit poem, 'Acchut ki Shikayat' (The Untouchable's Complaint), distinctly placed Dalit experiences on the literary map of the Indian sub-continent. Likewise, Achyutanand, in 1927, galvanized the possibilities of literature to raise critical questions against the Manusmriti, the keystone of Brahmanical casteism. One can even find the primal echoes of Dalit-feminist voices in the Buddhist literature of the Theras and Theris, composed nearly two millennia ago. The same might be said for the literature of the Siddha and Natha traditions. Collectively in all these writings, writers of Dalit and marginalized-caste backgrounds have played foundational roles, which are all important to recall as the ancestors of contemporary Dalit-feminism.

In collective memory only that literature truly abides, which raises substantive questions about (in)justice. The question of justice is raised and rendered in acutely sophisticated ways in Buddhist literature. Ashvaghosha (the author of epic-poems in Sanskrit like the Buddhacharita and Saundarananda) believed that injustice makes a person infirm, indisposed and ill. "A Brahman is born from the mouth, from the arms, the Kshatriya, the Vaishya from the thigh and the Shudra from the feet" – such visualizations of caste present in the RigVedic hymn of the 'primal man' (purusha), for instance, are completely unnatural. Humans are all always born the same way. It is the caste system – composed of the twin, intersecting systems of varna (colour) and jati (occupational status) – that are therefore truly unnatural and unscientific. They truly make one ill, debilitated, sick and (physically and socially) disabled. To be free from these afflictions, one needs to be medicated. Such a medicine is bitter but it promises to cure the ailing life. To counter the bitterness of the medicine, a dash of honey becomes necessary. Dalit writing and dissemination performs a vital, curative function. Dalit literature is therefore based on the test of logic and the incontrovertible veridiction of the everyday experiences of India's oppressed castes.

In contemporary times, the question of justice especially at it pertains to India's most marginalized communities came up substantively around the turn of the new millennium. Upholding the belief that injustice cannot be rooted-out on its own, and in the interest of building wider civic solidarities, Dalit-feminists, non-Dalit feminists, minorities etc. came together in critical ways around the year 2000. Dalit-feminists particularly came forward in large numbers and played a crucial role in creating these intersectional solidarities, especially since they were women from the lowest rungs of the caste system for whom the search for justice was essential both for their survival and existence. The intimate experience of injustice catalyzes the real search for equity. In the context of their 'double oppression' through caste and gender, their anger was both scathing and justified. Drawing from their own context, and nourished and nurtured by their own embodied experiences, the literature of Dalit women was an actualization of their radical visions and quotidian negotiations. Dalit feminist literature thus grapples acutely with questions of history as much as it goads us to imagine (and inhabit) radical horizons of an anti-caste futurity (including the challenges and contradictions that lie in its wake). In the same way, the anger (and at times, the anguish) we see in Kalyani Thakur's poems is anchored in the actuality of her experiences as a Dalit woman; it isn't an anger that is merely reactionary or righteous. Equally, it affirms itself through a careful and critical reflexivity, attentive all-along to the power, potential, possibilities and paradoxes of its own positionality.

Let us briefly examine how this all plays out in Kalyani Thakur's poetry. In her poem, 'The Fat Cat Gets the Cream, Always', the poet becomes the voice of those Dalits who seek to initiate revolution in the name of the land they've tilled as slaves for centuries, yet without ever having any control (or say) in its ownership. Innumerable generations of their families have come and gone yet they have never been able to own any land. They have only functioned as 'vote banks' from whom value is extracted without redistributive justice. They live on boiled rice-water; they don't know the flavour of food despite being the growers of grain. Yet, whenever there is a struggle, be it Nandigram, Singur or Marichjhapi, they are always the ones who get shot by the bullet, who really agitate - not the 'upper caste' Bhadralok. This seething sentiment is crystallized equally urgently in another poem, 'Wounded ideology', where Kalyani Thakur writes, "Leaders will forget their ideology/

We know, yet still follow them/Leaders of labour movements buy their success/With our labour as their capital/ Dalit sympathizers capitalize/On Dalit-lives."

Kalyani Thakur's crackling and captivating oeuvre is thus intensely inundated with Ambedkarite idea(l)s, which expose Brahmanical society as much as they open-up Dalit being to deeper, critical scrutiny. Her anger is most emphatic against the suffering and suppression of women. She writes equally forcefully about love, intimacy, male-female relations, and the everyday labour(s) of womanhood in a social world where Dalit women's experiences are silenced even by savarna feminists. Her poems particularly shore-up the depths of Dalit-feminist collective memory, whether in Bengal (through its histories of partition) or in the sub-continent at-large. In, 'The Burning', for instance, the poet pens a parable of the Chandal, the 'low caste' woman who must labour in the 'upper-caste' cremation grounds, performing caregiving's final gesture in spite of being segregated by the same system. "Having lit the sandalwood pyre/the fiery Chandal has left at the end of the day/sitting in the fragrant fire/an endless pain is mine/This is a strange taste."

Kalyani Thakur's writing is equally steeped in a stance of wonder, curiosity and concern for nature. Her poetry and imagery (re)affirm the vitality and vigour of an everyday humanism, in which one's commitments to the preservation of history cannot be divorced from the forces of nature (in which one's ancestors dwell). She writes, "You are the human who has forgotten the smell of the soil/ amidst the many domes and pillars of the big city/ You have lost your green heart that walked through/ the green fields." Hers then becomes the essential voice of a distinctive Dalit-feminist ecocriticism. Equally, she reveals how 'upper-castes' appropriate the vagaries of nature to uphold the caste structure. When a famine strikes the land, the King condescendingly scatters some rice grain for his subjects. The "rice slaves", however, enfeebled by hunger and incarcerated by caste cannot revolt. Their fate is well known even to the King. On the verge of starvation, the poet writes, "And some are so engaged in licking their fingers/that they grow quite unmindful/of raising their clenched fists to the skies/in protest."

Kalyani Thakur's Dalit-feminist poems further also direct their attention towards adivasi, who live deep in the forest. Their children are born and live chronically with malnutrition, whilst they, our tribal brethren, slave and sweat in the service of the state, which is slowly but surely exploiting and exterminating them. "The green fields of grass turn red/ with the blood of the black men/ of Jungle-Mahal", writes Kalyani Thakur in the poem 'Lalgarh', a succinct yet searing chronicle about the tribulations of a small tribal village caught in the crossfire of competing political interests.

The complex relationship between the exploiters and exploited, which always forms a key subtext of Kalyani Thakur's writing thus becomes the foundational canvas of her layered reflections on caste. She has written, "Like the bait hanging off the end of a fishing-rod, our Dalit society still dangles in a precarious position, sometimes it becomes Ambedkarite, sometimes it turns in completely the opposite direction; it is yet to emerge from its own vacillations." As a result, the writer argues, it is difficult to ascertain when (and how) Dalits will be able to course-correct within the Brahmanical system of oppression(s). This is a form of critical concern and care towards Dalits. Another crucial aspect of Babasaheb Ambedkar's radical vision pertained to the feminist question: that men and women are equal in the home and outside. Yet, implicit and explicit patriarchal biases towards women and girls remains rife in India's caste-hierarchies even today. In her poem, 'The Shoe-Society', Kalyani Thakur urges women to lay claim on the world whilst being critically attentive to the world-annihilating forces of caste: "Just as the foot inserts itself with care/ into the new leather shoe/ feeling its way forward gingerly/ Dear girl, make your own space/within this society carefully,/ cautiously feeling your way forward/ for it is as hard and inflexible as the shoe."

Babasaheb Ambedkar also secured for us all the right to vote, on the basis of which anyone can be capable of wielding substantive power in a democracy. The radical possibilities of universal adult franchise, however, can truly be achieved only when Dalits (and non-Dalits) exercise their collective authority in achieving Ambedkar's dream of annihilating caste. In her poem, 'Towards you, Babasaheb', Kalyani Thakur radically envisions this. There is a procession of "people flowing by like an unending stream" before whom she (the poet) picks-up a flagstaff. This gesture, which combines the power of Dalit feminist witnessing with its potential to re-engineer social equations fuels the peerless dream of an anti-caste future: "one by one/in slow but sure succession/more flags get picked up from the street side/ and we begin to walk", writes the poet.

Ambedkar's blue flag is now being raised and people all around are beginning to recognize and understand its significance. As Kalyani Thakur's poems tell us, Marxism and Brahmanism have both summarily failed to engender equitable visions of the future (indeed, even of the past). To imagine and instantiate humanism, she argues, one must (re)turn to the humanity of Babasaheb Ambedkar and his

Dalit sisters. This is the kind of striking consciousness and clarity that animates her poetry. For thousands of years, the society that was asleep, Kalyani Thakur exhorts them to awaken, agitate and truly
become the response Babasaheb Ambedkar sought to cultivate against the grisliness of caste and gender oppression. It is my firm belief that the reader will heed her sterling, humanist clarion-call.

Translated from Hindi by Nikhil Pandhi

**From *The Girl Who Tracks the Dark /
Aandhare O Meye***

1. THE-GIRL-WHO-TRACKS-THE-DARK / AANDHARE O MEYE

WHISPER INTO THE EARS OF THE MOONSHINE ABOUT:
> THE-GIRL-WHO-TRACKS-THE-DARK

EVEN THE FIREFLY KNOWS OF
THE-GIRL-IN-THE-CORNERS-OF-THE-ROOM

THE DEER, FRIENDS TO
THE-GIRL-WHO-BREAKS-WORDS

THE CLOUDS KNOW OF HER HURT
THE-GIRL-WHO-IS-DRENCHED-IN-RAIN.

SHE'S
THE-GIRL-WHO-SWIMS-AGAINST-THE-CURRENT

HER BOAT HAS A TATTERED SAIL IN AUTUMNAL STORMS

THE-GIRL-WHO-GRINDS-THE-SPICES
HAS THE MORTAR AND PESTLE
                FOR HER COMPANIONS.
THE SPICES KNOW HER LANGUAGE,
THE GINGER,
THE POPPY,
THE CHILLI
            AND
THE CUMIN.

FASCINATING SHE SEEMS,
THIS
    TOUGH-UP-GIRL

WIPING SWEAT OFF HER BROW
LIFTING UP THE PLOUGH,
THIS
    JEWEL-IN-THE-DARK.

Translated by Sipra Mukherjee

2. RICE-SLAVES / ANNA DĀSH

As a result of the famine's cause and
consequence, the King and his subjects
confront each other. The King scatters some
rice grains from his repository, his subjects
begin to feed on the given grains.
And some are so engaged in licking their
fingers that they grow quite unmindful
        of raising their clenched fists
                to the skies in protest

Translated by Sipra Mukherjee

3. YOU WHO HAVE FORGOTTEN THE SMELL OF THE SOIL /
MATIR GANDHO BHULE JAOA MANUSH

You are the human who has forgotten the
     smell of the soil
amid the many domes and pillars of the big
city You have lost your green heart that
walked the pastoral paths

Pumpkins, squashes, and cabbages are lost
amid cakes, pastries, patties
and Chinese takeout

No more koyels and swallows, your dawn is
heralded via another molecular smell, your
mornings arrive not on the wings of bees,
your seasons change
in the luxury of air-conditioned hotel
rooms on distant seashores

You who have forgotten the smell of the
soil, I know you've forgotten those tunes
Bhatiyali, Kabi or the Baul, if so let the past days
be replete with
the errant fragrance-resonance-drunkenness

Translated by Mrinmoy Pramanick

4. POETRY IS AUCTIONED OFF / KABITA NILAME BIKOY

I strip myself naked to give all
at the feet of my poetry

Collecting them between two covers
I carry my poems to the market

In that dust-filled bazaar
my poetry is traded

And all are auctioned off,
myself, and the burden of my poems

Translated by Sipra Mukherjee

5. LYRICS OF LOVE AND LUST / ANU KABITA

1

Nobody wants to hurt somebody else
yet we all injure each other in silence

2

You can argue all you want, but I know
even the vagina forgets the lust-night

3

I have never exposed my breakings to
anyone only the damp pillow knows
everything

4

I myself dig a pond of melancholia
and then bathe in it every day and night

5

All the fires turn into vapour
in the stream of ice-cold water

6

We meet, though we hardly speak
Just that we often share our pains

Translated by Mrinmoy Pramanick

6. NOT SO VERY GOOD / TOTO BHALO NOI

I am not so very good
as to lend you some from my store
   of goodness
      and wash away your evil.

Would I, otherwise, have sat today
   in Ravana's Ashoka grove
condemning Raghava, who knows only
filial piety and devotion to his subjects?

   Being a Sita of today, can I
      be so much of a Sati?

   Let me therefore repeat,
   I am not so very good
as to lend you some from my store
   of goodness
      and wash away your evil.

Translated by Sipra Mukherjee

Note: Raghava is another name of Rama

7. COME LET US TALK OF PEACE / ESHO SANDHIR KATHA BOLI

I talk of war
    I talk of peace

My dear lover, come, let us
    talk of life

For the sake of our future generations
    let us talk of mutual peace

Translated by Sipra Mukherjee

8. THIS UNSKILLED POTTER / APATU KUMOR EK

All is crumbling to ruins around me
and yet I sit, an unskilled potter,
    with fresh clay in my hands

The restless potter's wheel spins

    Some pots and pans, some tongs
    and ladles break as I arrange them in
    the sun
even before I can put them to the fire

Yet I sit with fresh clay in my hands,
    an unskilled potter.

Translated by Sipra Mukherjee

9. WOULD I EVER HAVE KNOWN / KOKHONO KI JANTE PARTAM

Would I ever have known
in my entire life that I carry within me
such a big rain-laden cloud

One that can flood a river
and turn it into an ocean

Had you not come today and then gone
away would I ever have known
such pouring rains

Translated by Sipra Mukherjee

10. THE BURNING / DAHAN

Having lit the sandalwood pyre
the fiery Chandal has left at the end of the day

sitting in the fragrant fire
an endless pain is mine

This is a strange taste
the thought bringing pleasure and relief
that somebody has cremated and left.

In this unfamiliar, deserted shamsan
there is nothing for me to do.

Translated by Sipra Mukherjee

Note: Shamsan: cremation ground

11. THE FAT CATS GET THE CREAM, ALWAYS / NEPORA DOI MARE CHIROKAL

Forgive me,
        but I cannot stand like you
                at the back of this long procession
                    and lend my voice
        Those of you who seek to save the farmers' lands,
            or campaign for industrialisation,

I wonder, did any of your
fourteen generations ever farm?

                            To both of you,
                            the farmer is a
                            vote bank

Kindly do not confuse
these simple-minded
working-class humans with
your confounding theories

                        Do not bewilder
                        them regarding
                their status   Let them
                think through their own
                        problems

Those who do not know
which grain grows from
which seed,

or how many times
the reaped grain must
be steamed to make
the rice edible

Those who have only lived off
the fine-grained rice
harvested by these farmers,

Will those
bourgeois revolutionaries
please step aside?

Revolutions may happen
according to your whims But
the bullet hits the Nandigram villager
and it is the Nandigram resident who
goes to jail

The bhadralok
have never been hit
by bullets. And they
never will be —.

They will receive medals when
convenient and later, when convenient,
refuse the medals with great fanfare

But for whose progress
and whose benefit?

For those from Nandigram,
from Singur, for my kin,
bereaved at Marichjhapi,*
I can do nothing
but wet the pillow with tears —

My people, when
will you realise
that you are not of this land

Your vote
is all they care about,
the longer you take to comprehend this,
the more the lives that –

In all the riots,
in all the battles
that rage upon this land
It is only the Dalit
and the Muslim
who dies

Be it Godhra, or Singur
Or be it Nandigram*

And, meanwhile,
the fat cats steal all the cream.

Translated by Sipra Mukherjee

* Godhra is in Gujarat, known for recent communal riots. The others
are sites of peasant resistance against government or corporate appropri-
ation of land in West Bengal.

12. THEY WHO HAVE NO KING / JE JATIR RAJA NEI

For two hundred years you have tried
        To erase the names of
        Harichand, Guruchand
    Today, to their followers,
    You hold out your vote-beggar's hand   It fills
    me with contempt
How much longer will you deceive them?
    Wait, Matua brother, in the name of our
    Harichand Thakur   Let not a single vote go
    elsewhere   Send this message to every door:
        We want no plough, no land,
First, a King from amongst us; let your roar be
    'Our votes, our rule.'

Translated by Sipra Mukherjee

Note: Harichand and Guruchand were the leaders of a grassroots religious movement in eastern India which led to the political mobilisation and empowerment of a community that had been deemed lowly by social elites.

13. ON THE INSIDE / BHITAR PANE

You looked at my face
dew damp with views
barely knowing the thousands
of rains already poured down inside

Translated by Mrinmoy Pramanick

14. TOWARDS YOU, BABASAHEB / BABASAHEB TOMAR DIKE

For long I watched
    A few flags lying by the road
No rain or sun touched them
Or faded their colours
The people flowing by like an unending
stream
Paid scant attention
And so, fearing termites would get to the
flagstaffs I hoisted them onto my shoulders
and began walking
  And thence began the questions

But I lifted them up because you did not, I
say, and then I see
one by one,
in slow but sure succession,
more flags get picked up from the street side
and we begin to walk
    Which way lies the road?
Clueless at first, there're hesitations and
dithering
Some stray this way or that

Till finally we see
It is in one direction that we all have to go -- ....

Note:

Babasaheb: Dr Bhimrao Ramji Ambedkar, the father of the Indian Constitution and the Dalit leader known endearingly as Babasaheb.

From *Chandalini's Poetry /*
Chandalinir Kabita

15. CHANDALINI'S POETRY 11 / CHANDALINIR KABITA – 11

for all

I long for liberty

Hence, I sail this boat alone

I wish to go across borders and nations

I sail my little beyond rivers and oceans

No guards there at these borders

My boat from one shore to another

ferrying those that long

for liberty

Translated by Mrinmoy Pramanick

Note:

Chandalini: girl of the Chandala caste, a group deemed 'untouchable' in Brahminical Hinduism.

16. CHANDALINI'S POETRY 1 / CHANDALINIR KABITA – 1

"Let them do as they will."

"What is it to us?"

Leaders forget their ideology. We know, yet we still
follow them. Labour leaders buy their success with
our labour as their capital. Dalit sympathisers make
fodder of Dalit lives. Yet we believe in the veneer
of ideology.   The hopeful mind is hurt. Labour
and Dalits remain at the same status. Leaders
compromise with the masters, with Dalit-haters, and
buy their success   We clap for the leaders,
knowingly or unknowingly   It is a sad, roguish,
knavish time that hurts us. The bhadralok mind
accepts all quiet cheatings, compromises, petty
interests.   Why protest! Why bother
about the scams!
"Let them do as they will. What is it to us? It's the
government's job!" Alas, Government! Who? They
don't show   say all opportunist friends of mine.
    Yet I smile toothy, make small talk
    with them in great intimacy

"It's the government's job!"

Translated by Mrinmoy Pramanick

17. CHANDALINI'S POETRY 2 / CHANDALINIR KABITA - 2

I am leaving this riverbank

I am leaving the people of this jungle I

am walking to my faraway kin

leaving this river, forest and path

People, shedding their sweat and blood
  People, beaten up every day
  My ancestors

My children, struck with malnutrition
  My brothers and sisters,
  hunger-threatened, My relatives, my
  people, to them

I will go to them
  crossing - *four rivers*
  leaving - *five towns and villages.*

Translated by Mrinmoy Pramanick

18. CHANDALINI'S POETRY 12 / CHANDALINIR KABITA – 12

The moon falls down on my bed
If I smear his moonlight-pollen
If my fond desires pick up loves
          In this deep night, I am alone
          with the moon, windows wide open
          He enters without permission
In the zenana of a silent palace
the dream woman longs for her prince
But my moon pours out his desires
breaking the darkness on my bed

Translated by Mrinmoy Pramanick

19. CHANDALINI'S POETRY 16 / CHANDALINIR KABITA – 16

- Those who do not think of their country
- Those who do not think of their society
- Those who think only about their success
- Those who think only about their children

Please do not tell me to be like them,
Ma… Even the stairs of success may be
worm-eaten!

Translated by Mrinmoy Pramanick

20. CHANDALINI'S POETRY 24 / CHANDALINIR KABITA – 24

This is a spectacular game

Lalgarh, Lalgarh

A game between the green and the red

The blood of the black men
turns
the green grass
of Jungle-Mahal
red

Such a stunning game is this
between the Green and the Red

Translated by Mrinmoy Pramanick

This is a spectacular game

Such a stunning game is this

Notes:

Jungle Mahal: the political name of the forest region of the western part of West Bengal, mainly inhabited by Adivasis.

Lalgarh: a small village in the Jungle Mahal region. Many of the Adivasis and others here were killed due to political conflicts and state intervention.

Green and Red: The colours of the two political parties that currently hold sway in the state of West Bengal. Red is for the Communist Party, Green for the Trinamool Congress Party.

21. CHANDALINI'S POETRY 44 / CHANDALINIR KABITA – 44

I belong to nowhere
I do not have any flag
No flag is raised here
on 26th January
I am a woman from
    Chhitmahal at the border
of a broken Bengal, I belong
    to neither East nor West
Let me tell you
I do not have the right to vote, I do not
    have any state or leader

Ma is weeping, broken Ma
I am in between riots, and
religious-fanatics, From a no-citizen's
land
I am a woman from Chhitmahal
    Would you please listen to me
Would you please rejoin the lands
Would you please remove the barbed wire

Otherwise, give us the shelter called home
    Give us each a flag to raise!

Translated by Mrinmoy Pramanick

Notes:

Chhitmahal: The enclaves of the Indian nation that are geographically situated within alien territory. Due to the unfeasible and unrealistic border that was drawn between Pakistan and India by the British at the time of Partition, some inhabited land of India fell within the territory of East Pakistan (now Bangladesh), and vice versa.

From *Every Night Knows /*
Protiti Ratri Jane

22. AT THE END OF THE CENTURY / SHATEK SHESHE

Enveloped by a deep fog, our eyes had not yet
seen.
Only once the night was over would we know what
had passed on the other side in those hours

The time of danger is not yet past
perhaps The time to stand up tall
glimmers there,
in the distance, hidden behind the setting sun

Translated by Sipra Mukherjee

From the anthology Battle is Inevitable When We Meet / Dhorlei
Yuddha Sunishchit

**From *And She Returned Naked /
Phire Elo Ulanga Hoye***

◎

23. CLAIRVOYANCE / DOORADRISTI

The girl was a clairvoyant. She could foresee the storm
before the Weather Department did. She could
perceive the direction from which the enemy would
strike before the Foreign Affairs Ministry had even
sensed danger. Panicking, the ministers ran to
complain to the King.

The King wagged his head disapprovingly and said,
'This cannot be condoned. Get her here.'

So the King's men dragged her, bound and gagged,
to the King. 'Put her to death,' they demanded.

The King pondered for a while. Then said, 'Maybe not
just yet. But since she sees too much, gouge out her
far-seeing eyes.'

So they fired up the forge, got their iron daggers red
hot and thrust them into the girl's eyes. The girl
writhed in pain. But not a sound escaped her lips.
Reassured, the King settled back down to his usual
affairs. But within the week, his ministers came running
to him again.

◎

◎

'She doesn't see, yes. But another door of her mind
has opened. She speaks. She speaks of people
coming. Of people from the east, advancing
ceaselessly with unfurled flags and conch shell
trumpets. That boy. That boy they had sent from the
south – who we executed upon your orders. His
people too do not rest quiet. The clouds have
gathered over the forests. The skies are darkening.'

As the words fell on his ears, the King sensed a tremor
in the throne he sat upon. With increasing
desperation, the King began to shout instructions to
his ministers, flinging his words towards them as his
terror grew. But there was such chaos all around, that
nobody seemed able to hear him.

◎

Abridged, from the anthology And She Returned Naked / Phire Elo
Ulanga Hoye

From the anthology
The Battle is Inevitable When We Meet /
Dhorlei Yuddha Sunishchit

**From *The Horse Series /
Ashwa Series***

24. THE HORSE OF ASHWAMEDHA / ASHWAMEDHER GHODA

From the grave of Job Charnock
I plucked a flower and told you:
this is a memento of our friendship
Love was floating on a raft
Alas! Oh Behula, my dear, I knew from
our first night of marriage, this is the horse
of Ashwamedha, if you stop it, you must be
ready for war

Translated by Mrinmoy Pramanick

Notes:

Ashwamedha: one type of Hindu ritual. A king sends out a horse, and whatever land the horse covers will then belong to the king. If anybody stops the horse, they are preventing the king from occupying the land, who might then declare war.

Behula: a character from medieval Bengali narrative poems in Manasa Mangal. Behula was married to Lakhindar, son of rich trader Chand Sadagar. Manasa, the goddess of snakes, wanted to be recognised by a person who holds social power, and chose Chand Sadagar for this. A devotee of Lord Shiva, Chand refused to worship Manasa, who then sent a snake to bite Lakhinder on the first night of his marriage. Behula sailed in a raft with his body to heaven, where she persuaded the gods to give Lakhinder back his life, on the condition that Chand worship Manasa.

25. POETRY AGAINST WAR / JUDDHA BIRODHI KABITA

Sitting astride your white Pakshiraj
as we galloped along the Kargil border
    as we crossed the cities of Kabul,
    Kandahar, as we knelt before the
    Bamiyan Buddhas
  that had been raped, destroyed,
    asking for forgiveness
our heads bowed low with the shame of
    our naked civilizations

O Tathagata, the struggle you began
two and a half thousand years ago
    continues, even today —

    As we passed Israel, Palestine,
The flag in my hands changed colour
    again, and yet again,
from the tricolour to the green and red
    with the moon, to blue and red with white
    stars, and many many more such -
    and changing incessantly,
    seemingly at some point
it turned all white

And then at the farthest end of the earth
    we planted it, you and me,
    and started out
    in search of a new planet —

Translated by Sipra Mukherjee

Note:

Pakshiraj: A mythical winged horse.

26. THE DISOBEDIENT SOCIETY / BEYARA SAMAJ

The piteous broom tied at the waist
wipes out the footprints of the untouchable
    Yet the dalit will not be wiped out from this
    land despite burning
    for a thousand years
    So many are we

    In this land where narrow communalism
    disguises the evils of caste

  the docile civilised humans go
to their daily work, or raise a storm
    of words in their teacups --

So finally, I take to the busy streets
    a bell fastened to my staff

Taking the bridle of Time in hand
    I direct onto the right path
this disobedient stubborn horse,
    this worm-eaten society.

Translated by Sipra Mukherjee

**From *For Fear We Go Colour-Blind /
Paachhe Barnandha Hoye Jaai***

27. THE PROCESS OF CONSTRUCTION / GATHAN-PRANALI

Revealing the straw framework of the idol

is not the job of the sculptor.

But it is imperative to know

how the idol was built

The process of construction must be studied

As the imagined idea precedes reality

Or the beautiful before its reflection in the mirror

One must first love something

The straw-wood-rocks or a river

Translated by Sipra Mukherjee

Note:

The word 'colour' (varna) in the title of this anthology refers to the varna system of social stratification and discrimination first mentioned in the Vedas and persisting in Indian society to this day. Colourism, discrimination towards those with darker skin, is a significant feature.

28. TO CHUNI / CHUNI KE

My skin

dark so that I may know darkness

Your poets love the dark girl, calling her

'Krishnakali, Mriganayani.'

These eyes are not those of a gazelle,

but they are just as wary of predators

It is the lovers who bestow such epithets,

and to the lover-poets, I say,

rein in your self-indulgent effusions for dark girls

Paintings of perfect nude dark maidens sell

at high prices at auction houses

with the hammer's strike

My dears, tend to your dark Chunis with care

you don't want their anger and hurt

to bloom into red flowers of consciousness.

Translated by Sipra Mukherjee

Notes:

Chuni: Chuni Kotal was a young girl from the Lodha Sabar tribe who killed herself in 1992, unable to bear the constant humiliation and discrimination that she had to face as an Adivasi. She was the first woman to earn a Bachelor Honours degree from her tribe, and was studying for a Masters in Anthropology when she died. Her death led to the Dalits of West Bengal organising several protests and establishing the Bangla Dalit Sahitya Sanstha to resist and fight the evils of caste.

Krishnakali: A girl's name, meaning Dark flower. The reference is to a famous poem celebrating the beauty of a dark girl written by Rabindranath Tagore.

Mriganayani: A girl's name, meaning The One with the Deer's Eyes.

29. THE SHOE-SOCIETY / JUTO-SAMAJ

Just as the foot inserts itself with care

into the new leather shoe,

feeling its way forward gingerly

Dear girl, make your own space

within this society carefully,

cautiously feeling your way forward,

for it is as hard and inflexible as the shoe

If fortunate, you may find

by your side a Band-aid type

Baba or Big Bhai

If not, then within this hard-leather

society you will have to remain

blistered and burning, as you navigate

yet many more centuries

Translated by Sipra Mukherjee

30. OUR MANGALKAVYA / AMADER MANGALKAVYA

Sometimes I return,
I desire the ambitious past --
This life loves to flow like a stream
across all barriers

Let the stories of the Purana, Champakanagar be, let
the songs of Behula-sojourn be
We have never drowned in the shallow river
never sailed the boat on the Gangur

This society has bound you by
the ropes of Gandharva rule
Tear that fetter, keep your hand on mine
and let us gain our strength

Let us sing the Mangalgatha
in memory of a past we have torn and won

Translated by Mrinmoy Pramanick

Notes:

Mangalkavya: A corpus of Bengali religious texts devoted largely to deities who belong outside the pantheon of Vedic Hinduism. The Mangalkavyas, therefore, thought integral to Bengal's culture and literature, are the indigenous culture of communities who are outside the Brahminical hegemony.

Champaknagar: This was the town of Chand Sadagar, the trader who was a devotee of Shiva and contemptuous of the 'smaller' goddess Manasa, who is outside the pantheon of the Vedic deities.

Gangur: The river on which Behula sailed in order to reach the royal court of god Indra.

Gandharva: In Hindu, Buddhist and Jain mythology, celestial beings who are lesser than the gods and goddesses.

Mangalgatha: Ballads which sing of good wishes.

ENCORE

A ripple of quotes gathered from the collection

>   more flags get picked up from the street side
>   and we begin to walk

>   I will go to them
>   crossing

These eyes are not those of a gazelle

>   The time to stand up tall glimmers
>   there

One must first love something
The straw-wood-rocks or a river

Let us sing the Mangalgatha
in memory of a past we have torn and won

>   we planted it, you and me,
>   and started out
>   in search of a new planet

Dear girl, make your own space

>   So many are we

EDITORIAL NOTE

from Tice Cin

This translation of Kalyani Thakur Charal's poetry has spent a lot of time growing.

Especially in conversation.

It had a journey in editorial with editor Deborah Smith, translators Sipra Mukherjee, Mrinmoy Pramanick and poet Kalyani Thakur Charal. Then before a talk at SOAS University in London, Kristen Vida Alfaro and Kalyani spoke about the next stage of edits, one that could help her poems to be viewed in the context of the four books that they are taken from. She desired them to be received by an English-speaking audience, as political, incendiary and devotedly committed to community. Kalyani passed Kris pages with etchings on them, of new possibilities.

Through this, I was asked to come onto the editorial team for this book to winnow some of Kalyani's poems down upon her request, concentrating on bringing out this aspect of her poetry. My hope was to further honour Kalyani's original concepts (such as her numbering for particular titles) as well as holding conversations about creative copyediting with Abbas Jaffary. Our hope has always been to explore different things with our readership in the English-language, that includes the global Dalit community, activists and poets.

Speaking with Sipra, Kalyani, and Mrinmoy, we have renamed some translations to be called Chandalini's Poetry with numbers besides them, as Kalyani originally wrote them in the anthology *Chandalini Poetry / Chandalinir Kabita.* I asked why she uses numbers for some of her poems rather than titles and she told me, 'I think punctuation and names, these are exes of poetry. I do not think about it. The reader has intellect. They will think about it in their mind – let the reader think about the poetry and the meaning.' Meaning is everywhere. As stated in the Translators' Foreword, Kalyani is from the Dalit community that used to be called Chandals. The 'Charal' in Kalyani's name is an echo of that Chandal name. Translator Mrinmoy told me how this speaks to "the way she would be identified as a girl from that community". I asked Kalyani how she felt to claim that name, and she shared, "it makes me feel calm because the Chandal people are powerful. Beyond social exclusion they continued their oral tradition and culture – I am second generation literate – I am related with those women, chandalini. To those who wrote Charyapada [often regarded as the first book of Bengali literature]." Her autobiography *Ami Keno Charal Likhi* (*Why I Write Charal*) pertains to this too. We spoke longer as a group, and Kalyani then said, "every word I use, when I use Chandalini, I use to give myself the dignity of belonging to this community. A chandalini is an angry woman, we are using that word against the system. A resistance against a caste society.

Everything against." We spoke with Mrinmoy and Sipra of Tagore's Chandalika, his play on such a girl, of how her shadow couldn't even be touched.

Through this conversation we decided to add in and begin *I Belong to Nowhere* with a poem that Sipra, Mrinmoy and Kalyani felt would be a resonant representation of her works, the poem is called "The-girl-who-tracks-the-dark" stylised to look like a comic of sorts. Speaking with translator Sipra, she told me, "when I read the poem I looked upon it - this girl who carries a huge burden, capable of carrying a huge burden and moving forward with that. A creation and romanticization of this figure carrying a huge burden, kind of a mythmaking in the lines with shades of the super hero." There is an epic quality to it that we felt began a journey of poems on tracking and coursing through, like the "long procession" / 'michhil', that echoes throughout. A line of people walking down in protest. During calls with Sipra, Mrinmoy and Kalyani, we deepened our thoughts around the poems. We spoke of the poem 'The Fat Cats Get the Cream, Always / Nepora Doi Mare Chirokal ' and the bhadralok, and Mrinmoy spoke to me of the long history of bhadralok in West Bengal, a place where the term 'bourgeois' is also commonly used, "They are two classes - one is bhadralok and one is the down-trodden people (they are just expected to cast their vote without meaning to society).' This is especially prominent in the debate between industrialisation and land which should be saved – and as poignantly noted in the Translator's Foreword, 'they live on boiled rice-water; they don't know the flavour of food despite being the growers of grain'. The original title is an idiomatic phrase, 'Nepora

Doi Mare Chirokal' – which is roughly akin to, all the opportunists get the privileges and so the poem became, 'The Fat Cats Get the Cream, Always'.

There are depths to these lacks and aches of imbalance. The way that the full view of something is rarely seen, and instead a mirage of rain is reflected. In 'On the Inside/ Bhitar Pane', the poem speaks of seeing beyond what is reflected in the face, past those few drops of views. Beneath the surface. Of Abhimān. The person you expect love and understanding from. Words for a type of hurt love, some-one who is supposed to be empathetic to the narrator, but they are not understanding the depths of the individual. From the inside it is raining. We should know more.

My hope is that by the time you reach the encore on the final page, you see to the next layer of Kalyani's experience and of those who she writes about with conviction and passion. Her feminist and affirming call to her community.

ISBN (paperback)   9781911284765
ISBN (ebook)   9781911284758

A catalogue record for this book is available from the British Library.

Cover Art: Malvika Raj
Cover Design: Amandine Forest
Typesetting and Ebook Production: Abbas Jaffary, Jojy Philip
Editors: Tice Cin, Deborah Smith
Proofreader: Sophiya Ali
Acquiring Editor: Deborah Smith
Publicity: Nashwa Nasreldin, Hana Sandhu
Publishing Assistant: Nguyễn Đỗ Phương Anh
Rights Director: Julia Sanches
Commissioning Editor and Associate Art Director: Tice Cin
Publisher and Creative Director: Kristen Vida Alfaro

First Printing (2023)

Supported using public funding by
ARTS COUNCIL
ENGLAND

ABOUT TILTED AXIS PRESS

Tilted Axis publishes mainly work by Asian and African writers, translated into a variety of Englishes. This is an artistic project, for the benefit of readers who would not otherwise have access to the work – including ourselves. We publish what we find personally compelling.

Founded in 2015, we are based in the UK, a state whose former and current imperialism severely impacts writers in the majority world. This position, and those of our individual members, informs our practice, which is also an ongoing exploration into alternatives – to the hierarchisation of certain languages and forms, including forms of translation; to the monoculture of globalisation; to cultural, narrative, and visual stereotypes; to the commercialisation and celebrification of literature and literary translation.

We value the work of translation and translators through fair, transparent pay, public acknowledgement, and respectful communication. We are dedicated to improving access to the industry, through translator mentorships, paid publishing internships, open calls and guest curation.

Our publishing is a work in progress – we are always open to feedback, including constructive criticism, and suggestions for collaborations. We are particularly keen to connect with Black and indigenous translators of Asian and African languages.

tiltedaxispress.com

@TiltedAxisPress